JUNIOR
BIOGRAPHIES

VIOLA DAVIS

ACTRESS

Enslow Publishi
101 W. 23rd Street
Suite 240
New York, NY 10011
USA

enslow.com

...urgang

WORDS TO KNOW

debut A beginning.

groom To clean and take care of an animal.

inspired To be moved to do something.

minority A member of a smaller group that is different from the larger group. Differences may include race or sex.

nominated To be chosen as a possible winner of an award or honor.

protest A public event, like a march, at which people voice their disapproval of something.

racism The unfair treatment of people because of their race.

CONTENTS

MEDIA | D

LOS ANGELES

Viola Davis

CHAPTER 1

A YOUNG LIFE

Actress Viola Davis lights up the big screen in some of the most cherished Hollywood movies. She has played wives, mothers, and hired help. She has been in stories told in the past, in the present day, and even in the future. Viola's acting work has earned her many honors and awards. She is the first African American actress to be **nominated** for three Academy Awards for her work in films.

BEGINNINGS

Viola Davis was born on August 11, 1965, in St. Matthews, South Carolina. She was born on her grandmother's farm. She moved with her family to Central Falls, Rhode Island, when she was just two months old.

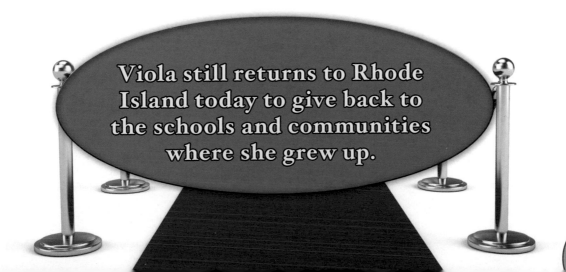

Viola still returns to Rhode Island today to give back to the schools and communities where she grew up.

Viola grew up in Central Falls, Rhode Island.

GROWING UP

Viola's family was very poor. The family did not have
enough money to move everyone to Rhode Island. Her
older sister and brother had to stay back on the farm with
their grandparents.

Viola's father groomed and trained horses. Her mother was a factory worker and a maid. Viola's mother was also very active in the civil rights movement, which began in the 1950s. This was a time when many people were beginning to fight back against unfair treatment of black people. When Viola was just two years old, her mother was arrested during a protest. Viola had to go to jail with her.

Viola Says:
"I would tell my younger self just be yourself— that who you are is good enough."

CHAPTER 2
BECOMING AN ACTOR

In high school, Viola became interested in theater. After she graduated, she studied acting at Rhode Island College. She also attended the Juilliard School of Performing Arts in New York City. Juilliard is very highly respected, and many well-known actors and performers have attended the school.

The greatest place to become known as an actor in New York City is on Broadway. Many of the theater shows there are world famous. Tourists from around the world go to Broadway to see shows. Viola made her **debut** on Broadway in 1996 in a play called *Seven Guitars*. Since then, she has won two Tony Awards for her work on Broadway. A Tony Award is the highest honor for acting in stage performances.

Academy Awards (also known as Oscars) are given for performances in movies. Emmy Awards are given for performances in television programs. Tony Awards are given for performances in Broadway shows.

Viola graduated from the Juilliard School in 1993. Here, she receives an honorary degree in fine arts from the school in 2014.

THE JOURNEY TO THE BIG SCREEN

After her work on Broadway, Viola decided to move on to television and film. She appeared on television dramas such as *City of Angels* and *Law & Order*. Years later, she went on to appear on the popular show *How to Get Away with Murder*. She became the first African American woman to receive an Emmy Award for Outstanding Lead Actress in a Drama Series. She also took smaller roles in films. In 2008, she was noticed for her small

Viola plays the role of Esther in the 2004 play *Intimate Apparel*.

but important role in the film *Doubt.* She received a nomination for an Academy Award.

SHINING A LIGHT ON RACISM

One of the most well-known roles that Viola played was a maid in the 2011 film *The Help.* The movie was based on a book of the same name. The story examines the racism African Americans faced during the 1960s. The film was nominated for an Academy Award for Best Picture. It helped bring attention to the issue of racism in America. It taught young people today how relations among black people and white people have changed and how they have stayed the same.

Viola Says:

"The women in [*The Help*] were like my mother, my grandmother. Women born and raised in the Deep South, working in tobacco and cotton fields, taking care of their kids and other people's kids, cleaning homes."

Viola plays the role of a maid in the film *The Help*.

The Help was not Viola's first performance dealing with racism. One of the plays for which she received a Tony Award when she was younger was called *Fences*. In 2016, Viola went on to play the same part on the big screen, along with her costar, Denzel Washington.

In 2017, Viola won an Academy Award for her role in *Fences*. The story is about an African American sanitation worker, Troy, played by Denzel Washington. Troy has dreams of becoming a baseball player but is not allowed to play because he is black. The story shows how difficult it was to be black in the 1950s. The film is based on the book *Fences*, by August Wilson.

Viola takes a bow with Denzel Washington, her costar in the stage and film versions of *Fences*.

Viola plays the wife in the story. She won an Academy Award for Best Supporting Actress for her role. In her acceptance speech, Viola dedicated her award to her father, who she says struggled in similar ways as the movie's main character, Troy.

RECORD-SETTING AWARDS

Winning the Academy Award made Viola a record-setter for the number of acting awards won by an African American actress. She is the first African American in history to earn three Oscar nominations. She is also the first African American to earn three different acting awards. She has won an Academy Award, an Emmy Award, and a Tony Award.

Viola Says:

"[My father] had a fifth-grade education and didn't know how to read until he was fifteen. But you know what? He had a story and it deserved to be told—and August Wilson told it."

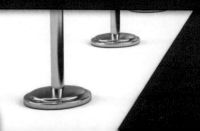

Viola celebrates winning the Academy Award for Best Actress in a Supporting Role for *Fences*.

Viola receives a star on the Hollywood Walk of Fame in January 2017. She is joined by her castmates from the TV show *How to Get Away with Murder.*

Viola's acting abilities have been noticed in all kinds of performances. She has the range of emotions needed to tell serious stories. The characters she plays are understood by people of all ages. Her performances help people understand different time periods.

Viola is married to an actor and Hollywood producer, Julius Tennon. The couple adopted a daughter named Genesis in 2011.

CHAPTER 4
A FUTURE IN HOLLYWOOD

Viola's work does more than just entertain people. It helps to change a problem that has existed in Hollywood for decades. The problem is that there are not as many stories told about African Americans and other **minorities** as there are about white people. Viola is part of the solution to this problem. She has helped increase the number of writers and directors who want to tell good stories about the African American experience. They see strong actors like Viola helping to tell their stories.

Viola has said that she would like to become a producer. She wants to find important stories herself instead of just waiting for good roles to come along.

Viola appears on *XQ Super School Live* in 2017. The program raised awareness about the need to improve public schools.

Viola with her husband, Julius Tennon, and their daughter, Genesis

Viola Says:

"I became an artist and thank God I did, because we are the only profession that celebrates what it means to live a life."

THE FUTURE FOR VIOLA

There is a bright future for Viola as an actor. After winning many awards, actors get to choose better and better roles. The future of Hollywood may even change because of the roles Viola takes. Just as she was **inspired** as a young actress to succeed, she may inspire other young actresses who want to go into the field of acting.

TIMELINE

1965 Viola Davis is born in South Carolina.
Moves to Rhode Island at two months old.

1967 Is sent to jail with her mother, who is arrested during a protest.

1988 Graduates from Rhode Island College.

1993 Graduates from the Juilliard School in New York City.

1996 Debuts on Broadway in *Seven Guitars*.

2007 Wins first Tony Award for her role in *King Hedley II*.

2008 Is nominated for Best Supporting Actress in *Doubt*.

2011 Wins Screen Actors Guild Award for Outstanding Performance by a Female Actor in a Leading Role for *The Help*.

2015 Wins Emmy Award for her role in *How to Get Away with Murder*.

2017 Wins an Academy Award for Best Actress in a Supporting Role for *Fences*.

BOOKS

Dabrowski, Kristen. *My First Acting Book.* Hanover, NH: Smith and Kraus, 2009.

Hooks, Gwendolyn, and Kelly Kennedy. *If You Were a Kid During the Civil Rights Movement.* New York, NY: Children's Press/Franklin Watts, 2017.

Kimmel, Mike. *Acting Scenes for Kids and Tweens.* New York, NY: Ben Rose Creative Arts, 2017.

WEBSITES

Screen Actors Guild

www.sagaftra.org/content/for-kids

Includes a special section for young performers that offers games, trivia, and a glossary for young people who want to learn about the acting business.

Viola Davis' Official Website

www.juveeproductions.com

Find the latest news about Viola, view photos, and learn about her charity work.

INDEX

Published in 2019 by Enslow Publishing, LLC.
101 W. 23rd Street, Suite 240, New York, NY 10011

Copyright © 2019 by Enslow Publishing, LLC.
All rights reserved.

No part of this book may be reproduced by any means without the written permission of the publisher.

Library of Congress Cataloging-in-Publication Data

Names: Furgang, Kathy, author.
Title: Viola Davis : actress / Kathy Furgang.
Description: New York : Enslow Publishing, 2019. | Series: Junior biographies | Audience: Grades 3-6| Includes bibliographical references and index.
Identifiers: LCCN 2017045639| ISBN 9780766097193 (library bound) | ISBN 9780766097209 (pbk.) | ISBN 9780766097216 (6 pack)
Subjects: LCSH: Davis, Viola, 1965—Juvenile literature. | Actors–United States–Juvenile literature.
Classification: LCC PN2287.D3225 F87 2017 | DDC 791.4302/8092 [B] –dc23
LC record available at https://lccn.loc.gov/2017045639

Printed in the United States of America

To Our Readers: We have done our best to make sure all website addresses in this book were active and appropriate when we went to press. However, the author and the publisher have no control over and assume no liability for the material available on those websites or on any websites they may link to. Any comments or suggestions can be sent by e-mail to customerservice@enslow.com.

Photo Credits: Cover, p. 1 Steve Granitz/WireImage/Getty Images; p. 4 Jason LaVeris/FilmMagic/Getty Images; p. 6 © AP Images; p. 9 Mike Coppola/Getty Images; p. 10 Anne Cusack/Los Angeles Times/Getty Images; p. 12 Moviestore collection Ltd/Alamy Stock Photo; p. 13 Jim Spellman/WireImage/Getty Images; p. 15 Jeffrey Mayer/WireImage/Getty Images; p. 16 Paul Archuleta/FilmMagic/Getty Images; p. 19 Tommaso Boddi/Getty Images; p. 20 Stefanie Keenan/Getty Images; interior page bottoms (red carpet) Sashkin/Shutterstock.com.